FANTASY IN LITERATURE

Fantasy in Literature

by John Aquino

National Education Association
Washington, D.C.

Copyright © 1977
National Education Association of the United States
Stock No. 1817-6-00 (paper)
        1818-4-00 (cloth)

Note

The opinions expressed in this publication should not be construed as representing the policy or position of the National Education Association. Materials published as part of the Developments in Classroom Instruction series are intended to be discussion documents for teachers who are concerned with specialized interests of the profession.

Library of Congress Cataloging in Publication Data

Aquino, John.
  Fantasy in literature

  (Developments in classroom instruction)
  Bibliography: p.
  1. Fantastic literature—Study and teaching. I
I. Title. II. Series.
PN56.F34A7   372.6′4   77-22178
ISBN 0-8106-1818-4
ISBN 0-8106-1817-6 pbk.

CONTENTS

1. Introduction

In the mid 1960s, fantasy literature became a fad. *The Lord of the Rings* was issued in paperback and became *the* book to read, especially on college campuses. Elementary and secondary school educators wrote articles advocating the Tolkien trilogy for class use. On buttons, bumper stickers, and walls, "Frodo Lives" proclaimed the relevance of the book's hero. Maps of Middle Earth, Tolkien calendars, and Tolkien societies proliferated. Ballantine Books, publishers of the authorized paperback edition, started an adult fantasy series of both modern and "classic" literature that explored fantastic, magical themes, and other publishers followed this trend.

The fantasy literature fad became less fanatic in the late 1970s, continuing in a more mature, established manner as courses in fantasy literature became part of many curriculums at the postsecondary, secondary, and even elementary levels.

But fantasy literature is not just the stuff of fads. It can easily be argued that fictional literature was in no way "realistic" until modern times. Aristophanes, Homer, Chaucer, Shakespeare, and even Ben Jonson dealt in some measure with the fantastic and fanciful. However, the eighteenth century brought the Age of Rationalism; and from that time on (allowing for some oversimplification) alternating trends for and against fantasy literature are in evidence. Horace Walpole reacted against the Age of Rationalism and wrote *The Castle of Otranto* in 1764, inaugurating the gothic novel. In the early nineteenth century the Romantic poets (especially Shelley and Keats) drew heavily on classical myths. Proper Victorian England was correct and conservative until advanced scientific inquiry undermined conventional thinking, and induced the birth of modern "pure" fantasy literature in the works of Lewis Carroll, William Morris, and George MacDonald. After the turn of the century fantasy literature prospered along with the Edwardian era in the works of James Barrie, Lord Dunsany, H. Rider Haggard, and others. But America in the late 1800s and early 1900s, struggling to create a literature from its own experience, produced mainly works that were predominantly naturalistic (Kate Chopin, Stephen Crane, Jack London, and Frank Norris).

In the twentieth century wars, depressions, and psychoanalysis turned literature away from fanciful imaginings, and caused development of the fear that fantasy literature might psychologically harm children. There were exceptions and reactions to this literary realism and this fear in the works of C. S. Lewis, Hugh Lofting, J. R. R. Tolkien, and Antoine de Saint-Exupery, who all wrote fantasy literature.

The prosperous postwar 1950s, which saw the initial publication of Tolkien's *The Lord of the Rings* and the growth of science fiction films, were followed by the science-oriented 1960s, which were shaped by sputniks, the Vietnam war, student riots, and crime in the streets. "Relevance" in children's literature and in schools became the fashion. Then, into the midst of this rational relevance came the paperback edition of *The Lord of the Rings* and the fantasy "fad," as well as an interest in the supernatural, in mysticism, and in modern witch cults.

Fantasy literature endures, although its position before the public, and consequently in education, has been erratic. But does it have any value as literature, especially within an educational setting? Is it possible to eliminate the objections of some educators to the violence and the lack of relevance of fantasy literature and the claims of some psychologists that fantasy of the mind must be regulated? Does the "wonder" that proponents of fantasy literature emphasize have real value?

The first part of this report will discuss the opposition as well as the support for fantasy both as an activity of the mind and as literature. The second part will present suggestions for teaching fantasy literature.

2. Fantasy as an Activity of the Mind

"Fantasy" is defined as "imagination, especially when extravagant and unrestricted . . . imaginative activity . . ."[1]

Because fantasy as an activity of the mind was often disparaged in the past, the fantasy or make-believe life of the learner in the educational process has received little attention until recent years. Samuel Johnson, for example, wrote in *Rasselas*, "All power of fantasy over reason is a degree of insanity."[2] Fantasy was often equated with its root word "fancy," of which Ralph Waldo Emerson wrote, "Men live in their fancy like drunkards whose hands are too soft and tremulous for successful labor."[3]

The neglect of fantasy in strictly psychological writings has been due both to a trend in early twentieth century American psychological thought away from introspective research,[4] and to interpretations of free-floating imagination as idle and possibly harmful reverie.[5] Sigmund Freud believed daydreams to be the product of unfulfilled needs and desires:

> The study of psychoneuroses leads to the surprising discovery that these phantasies and daydreams are the immediate forerunners of hysterical symptoms, or at least a whole number of them.[6]

Maria Montessori felt fantasy to be a "pathological tendency of early childhood."[7]

Other voices, however, have found value in fantasy, especially in recent times. For Jean Piaget, make-believe in child development is a presymbolic form of thought.[8] Erik H. Erikson held that play, generally a type of fantasy activity, is "the royal road to the understanding of the infantile ego's efforts at synthesis"[9] as well as "a function of the ego, an attempt to synchronize the bodily and the social processes with the self."[10] Bruno Bettelheim wrote that in both child and adult psychological harm can be done when the unconscious is repressed; however, when unconscious material is permitted to come to awareness and is worked through in imagination, its harmful potential is reduced, and some of its force can be made to serve positive purposes.[11]

Carl Jung, a one-time pupil of Freud, stated that because in our daily experience we have learned to discard the trimmings of fantasy in both our language and in our thoughts, a quality that is still characteristic of the primitive mind—and consequently, part of our being—has been lost.[12] William Wordsworth, writing in an earlier time and in verse, complained of the same loss:

> The world is too much with us: late and soon
> Getting and spending, we lay waste our powers;
> Little we see in nature that is ours . . .
> It moves us not.—Great God! I'd rather be
> A Pagan suckled in a creed outworn;
> So might I, standing on this pleasant lea,
> Have glimpses that would make me less forlorn,
> Have sight of Proteus rising from the sea
> Or hear old Triton blow his wreathed horn.[13]

For Jung, the recollection of infantile memories and the reproduction of archetypal ways of psychic behavior can create a wider horizon and a greater extension of consciousness.[14] For him, the fanciful imaginings of childhood are not worthless, rather their existence and their later assimilation and integration are essential for adult development. Again, Wordsworth anticipated Jung, seeing childhood thoughts as primal thoughts, as memories of a perfect, heavenly world:

> Our birth is but a sleep and a forgetting:
> The Soul that rises with us, our life's star,
>   Hath had elsewhere its setting,
>   And cometh from afar:
>   Not in entire forgetfulness,
>   And not in utter nakedness
> But trailing clouds of glory do we come
>   From God who is our home . . .
> At length the Man perceives it die away,
> And fade into the light of common day.[15]

And Wordsworth, like Jung, finds value in what one remembers, in what remains:

> O joy! that in our embers
> Is something that doth live,
> That nature yet remembers
> What was so fugitive . . .
> Those shadowy recollections
> Which be they what they may,
> Are yet the fountain light of all our day,
> Are yet a master light of all our seeing.[16]

Recent psychological research has provided documentation for the benefits of fantasy. Mary Ann Pulaski cited studies that indicate that children who have vivid and fanciful imaginations can sit quietly longer than less imaginative youngsters, are less aggressive, and tell more creative stories.[17] Jerome Bruner wrote that fantasy/play is a precursor of adult competence, providing the basis for useful problem solving and for language development.[18] Jerome Singer noted that if the fantasy life is not developed by adulthood, the individual tends to be less relaxed, less independent, and more bored than more imaginative people.[19] Fantasy, which has always

11

played a large part in literature (fairy stories, myth, folk takes, fiction in general), is now also seen as essential for the sciences; for without imagination and fantasy, chemistry and physics are denied new hypotheses, new methods of research, and the invention of new implements.[20] In short, fantasy is basic in human make-up and for human development.

Perhaps it is appropriate that the closing word about fantasy as an activity of the mind should come from a piece of fantasy literature, since this literature caters to this mental activity. In a Kahlil Gibran sketch, "The Goddess of Fantasy," the narrator encounters the goddess who compares herself to a metaphor embracing reality. She tells him that thoughts have a higher dwelling place than the visible world. The sketch concludes:

> And the Goddess of Fantasy drew me towards her with her magic glance and imprinted a kiss upon my burning lips and said, "Tell them he who passes not his days in the realm of dreams is the slave of the days."[21]

3. Fantasy Literature

Fantasy literature is defined by J. R. R. Tolkien as a specific genre that involves the creation of an imaginary other world,[22] an other world that is the land of faerie (by "faerie" Tolkien means magic).[23] Tolkien's definition also specifies complete subcreation of this other world (like his Middle Earth in *The Hobbit* and *The Lord of the Rings*). Although his specification of complete subcreation of an other world for fantasy literature eliminates stories of ancient gods on earth, stories that end as dreams, and all literature that has any base in reality, for the purposes of this report, which emphasizes elementary and secondary instruction, Tolkien's definition is expanded to encompass myths and fairy tales in addition to modern or "pure" fantasies. The term "fantasy literature," then, will refer to writings, usually fictions, that posit an imaginary other world.[24] Pure fantasy is distinguished from myth and fairy tales by not having oral origins; and it is distinguished from science fiction and other fantastic genres by having for its entire concern the creation of a believable other world.[25]

As there were negative reactions to fantasy as an activity of the mind, there have also been objections to the unreality of fantasy literature and the effect of this on children. Maria Montessori wrote:

> In the school, they [educationists] want children to learn dry facts of reality, while their imagination is cultivated by fairy tales, concerned with a world that is certainly full of marvels, but not the world around them in which they live. Certainly these tales have impressive factors which move the childish mind to pity and horror, for they are full of woe and tragedy, of children who are starved, ill-treated, abandoned, and betrayed. Just as adults find pleasure in tragic drama and literature, these tales of goblins and monsters give pleasure and stir the child's imagination, but they have no connection with reality.[26]

Walter Kerr, writing specifically about fantasy drama, noted that such drama is seldom great because it makes less of the world than the world actually is:

> But in point of fact a winged horse is less a horse than one without wings is. The horse has lost his own identity without acquiring a new one that is real. As he is not a true horse, he is not a true bird; he is not really a true anything. And the blithe dismissal of truth, pretty and playful though it may be, ends in a defeat of truth.[27]

Some writers and researchers have objected to fantasy literature because of the effect its violence and amorality can have on children. A. M. Tausch, for example, recorded a study in which children were observed during and after a reading of "Snow White," reporting that the fairy tale made an emotionally upsetting and ethically problematic impression on the children.[28] Stemming from this kind of criticism of fantasy literature, there was a trend in the early 1960s towards stories that dealt realistically with contemporary situations and problems.[29] Isabell Jan claimed that the modern fairy tale "has definitely had its day," and that the trend towards realism in children's literature came from the fact that children are no longer brought up by nurses in a nursery nor subject to compulsory public school lore. The deliberate unreality of these stories, according to Jan, "fails to satisfy children's imaginations while adults find them to be contorted."[30]

There have been, however, many defenders of fantasy literature who find that fantasy literature expresses something basic to humanity, and that fantasy literature involves universal, primitive truths essential to human development.

As an example of the defense, Bruno Bettelheim, who feels that fairy tales reveal truths about humanity, says:

> Fairy tales carry important messages to the conscious, the preconscious, and the unconscious mind, on whatever level each is functioning at the time. By dealing with universal human problems, particularly those which preoccupy the child's mind, these stories speak to his budding ego and encourage its development, while at the same time relieving preconscious and unconscious pressures.[31]

Some critics feel that psychoanalytical analysis of fairy tales and other fantasy literature can and has been overdone and is essentially extraliterary. But those who scoff at such analyses are perhaps too hasty; the belief that these stories exhibit universal truths and both conscious and unconscious thoughts seems often justified. The fairy tale "Beauty and the Beast," makes a useful illustration. Beauty, her father's favorite daughter, asks him for a white rose rather than a more costly present, quite unaware that she is asking too much. Her father steals the rose from the Beast's garden and is caught. The girl insists upon taking her father's punishment and goes to live in the enchanted castle with the Beast for three months. When her father grows ill, she secures permission to go to him; but because she delays her return to the Beast, she discovers he is dying for he cannot live without her. Beauty promises to wed him if only he will not die—and the Beast turns into a handsome prince. In analyzing this story, Joseph L. Henderson equates Beauty with any young girl or woman who has entered into an emotional bond with her father. Her request for a rose shows that she is at once innocent and unreasonable. She must break away from her father. By learning to love the Beast, Beauty awakens to the power of human love in its animal but also genuinely erotic form.[32] Such an analysis can be supported by specific reference to the story. But whether one agrees with it or not, the analysis serves to confirm Tolkien's claim in "On Fairy Stories" that fantasy literature is not trivial stuff but must instead be taken quite seriously.

Fantasy literature can also be taken seriously on a more conscious level. In Lewis Carroll's *Through the Looking Glass*, Alice, who is dreaming, meets Tweedledum and Tweedledee and while talking to them sees the Red King sleeping. Tweedledee tells Alice that the Red King is dreaming about her. " 'If that there King was to wake,' added Tweedledum, 'you'd go out—bang!—just like a candle!' " Tweedledum concludes that Alice is something in a dream and therefore not real. When Alice begins to cry and claims that the tears prove she is flesh and blood, Tweedledum says contemptuously, " 'I hope you don't suppose those are *real* tears?' " This discussion of what is real is a serious and even horrifying business for young Alice, and may be a necessary learning experience for both her and the young reader. This episode also includes a mirror-like regression—Alice dreams of the Red King, who is dreaming of Alice, who is dreaming of the Red King, who is dreaming of Alice, and so on into infinity.[33] The entire sequence is a good example of how fantasy literature deals with serious matters on a simple level.

C. S. Lewis praised fantasy literature for providing healthy developmental impetus for a child's mind. A typical children's story, he wrote, offers wish fulfilment that is compensatory, ravenous, and unrequited; but a fairy tale stirs and troubles the child with a sense of something beyond his/her reach, and, rather than dulling or emptying the actual world, gives it a new dimension.[34]

G. K. Chesterton presented a case that fairy tales demonstrate hard but healthy principles for child development:

> There is the chivalrous lesson of *Jack the Giant Killer* that giants should be killed because they are gigantic. . . . There is the great lesson of *Beauty and the Beast* that a thing must be loved before it is lovable. There is the terrible allegory of *The Sleeping Beauty*, which tells how the human creature was blessed with all birthday gifts, yet cursed with death; and how death may also be softened to a sleep.[35]

Bettelheim claimed that fairy tales "speak about his [the child's] severe inner pressures in a way that the child unconsciously understands, and . . . offer examples of both temporary and permanent solutions to pressing difficulties."[36]

In answer to those who claim that fantasy literature is "unrealistic" and therefore confusing to a child and detrimental to her/his development, Lewis wrote, "He does not despise the real woods because he has read of enchanted woods; the reading makes all woods enchanted."[37] Tolkien added, "If men really could not distinguish between frogs and men, fairy stories about frog kings would not have been written."[38]

To the critics who argue that fantasy literature is too violent and of no relevance to life, Lewis replied, "Since it is likely that they [children] will meet cruel enemies, let them at least have heard of knights and heroic courage."[39] Bettelheim offered the opinion that reactions against fairy tales stem from our desire to have children believe that all people are good and our refusal to let children know that the source of much that goes wrong in life is due to their own nature.[40]

The proponents of fantasy literature, and of its use by children, feel that within fantasy literature is real human experience, although it appears as the stuff of a dream or from the primal unconscious, or as universal truths and maxims, isolated, sketched in bold relief, simply but not childishly presented.

The criticism that fantasy literature is not true is at once correct and incorrect. It is true because it deals with human experience and because its action, as Tolkien would have it, is portrayed as convincingly as possible—in other words, as true.[41] Fantasy literature is true because it is the truth of our imagination.[42] And, it is not true because of the location of the story in the land of faerie. Through fantasy literature, children can learn what frogs are and what men are, learn which way is up because it is the way witches fly, and learn which way is down because that is where Humpty Dumpty falls. Fantasy literature, based on the premise "what if," introduces the child to the wonders of inquiry.

What of the value of fantasy literature as literature? In truth, in childhood education, the primary concern is with the child's overall development and not with the literary greatness of materials. But the language arts educator must admit that fantasy literature as a whole has advantages over "realistic" children's stories or the basal reader. Realistic fiction is, after all, relatively new, fantasy literature being 4,000 years older. Such varied works as Aristophanes's *The Birds*, Malory's *Morte d'Arthur*, Shakespeare's *A Midsummer Night's Dream*, Ann Radcliffe's *Mysteries of Udolpho*, Mark Twain's *A Connecticut Yankee in King Arthur's Court*, Kafka's *The Trial*, Shaw's *Man and Superman* and *Saint Joan*, Isak Dinesen's *Seven Gothic Tales*, and John Fowles's *The Magus* have characteristics of fantasy literature. Fantasy literature somewhat blatantly exposes children to the basic characteristic of all fictive literature: it has been made up. It is not real, and yet it is portrayed as true. Lang and Tolkien both noted that children constantly ask, "Is it true?"[43] an appropriate initial reaction to any fictive work.

Fantasy literature has an impressive collection of writings going back to ancient times. It often requires its writers to present a realistic unreality in extensive descriptive passages that can serve as a resource for language arts educators in introducing metaphor, simile, irony, paradox, and other literary techniques. It is a base from which young people can start to learn what literature is.

Northrop Frye, using Jungian terms, found fantasy literature basic to all literature and to a student's literature education:

As the student gets older, he reads more complicated literature, and this usually means literature concerned largely or exclusively with human situations and conflicts. The old primitive associations of human and natural worlds is still there in the background, but in, say, a novel of Henry James it's a long way in the background. We often feel that certain types of literature, such as fairy tales, are somehow good for the imagination: the reason is that they restore the primitive perspective that mythology has.[44]

Accordingly, Frye's recommended educational sequence, the primary stratum for teaching literature, is the Bible followed by mythology.[45]

Conclusion

Fantasy literature has often been criticized as an educational tool, and fantasy of the mind has often been disparaged. But just as often, the use of fantasy literature in education has been supported. Fantasy as an activity of the mind and consequently fantasy literature, which arises from and supports this activity of the mind, are felt to be essential to human development. Fantasy literature is also seen as useful in both language development and literature appreciation.

4. Teaching Fantasy Literature

This section offers possible approaches for teaching fantasy literature. Complete lesson plans for each class or each grade level are not presented, but rather suggestions that the teacher can adopt or can complement with other readings and activities in the same vein. For more extensive course descriptions, the reader is referred to the curriculum series from the University of Nebraska Curriculum Development Center, which, influenced by Frye's theories, is designed to lead the student from an apprehension of the "mythic" and anthropomorphic to an awareness of the realistic and analytic.

Developing Fantasy of the Mind

The use of fantasy literature in education presupposes the importance of fantasy as an activity of the mind. It is important, then, for a teacher to be concerned with the development of the fantasy life of her/his students.

For young children six and under, fantasy as an activity of the mind is readily ascertained because they show their imagination in observable play. A teacher can channel the development of their fantasies through pretend games, such as going on make-believe voyages or picnics, that can be supplemented by both reading aloud and story telling. In reading and telling, the teacher—and later the students—can employ different vocalizations to create the different roles and characters. The stories read and told can be embellished and re-created in make-believe play. The children's own personal fantasies can also be the subject for make-believe play activity, both individually and in groups, in the form of art, plays, pantomime, and song. Such play activity may serve as a form of release, or means of dissipating fear and distrust; but the teacher should control such fantasy or play activity within the limits of the classroom and should emphasize the positive aspects of individual control.

After approximately eight years of age, the fantasy life of students has changed—make-believe games are less acceptable socially. By this age children have generally achieved a firmer grasp of what is "real" and what is not.

But it is necessary to remember that the fantasy life of the individual child of any age is important, and will continue to be so for the rest of her or his life. Fantasy should always be available to provide answers for such questions as, What should I have done? What can I do? Is this what I should have said? Fantasy futures, expressed in such statements as, If I had the money, I would go to Spain and live in a castle, continue to be projected and developed. Films and televisions cater to ongoing fantasy living. Organizations such as the Society for Creative Anachronism, whose members wear medieval costumes and engage in jousts, re-create the legendary days of yore when life was supposedly freer and merrier.

Role playing, which requires all ages of students to imagine possible and impossible actions, individuals, and situations, is a recognized instructional method. These fantasy/play activities, important educational activities in themselves, can also be used to supplement fantasy literature instruction.

Characteristics of Fantasy Literature

Fantasy literature, which in this report is defined as writings, usually fictions, that posit an imaginary, magical, or "faerie" other world, has its roots in myths and fairy tales. These myths and fairy tales, which originate in oral traditions and reflect particular cultures, come to us in various secondhand transcriptions that are valuable as sources for later-crafted or "pure" fantasy literature and that are especially useful introductory material for a fantasy literature class.

The distinction between fairy tales and myths is sometimes unclear, although as a general rule fairy tales are characterized by happy endings, and myths can be characterized as having tragic or at least open-ended conclusions. Myths were born of fear of the unknown and a quest for order in the universe. They are how the ancients explained their world. The darkness of dusk was the cloak of a goddess covering the world. Willows seemed to weep beside lakes because they were transformed maidens mourning their drowned loves. Thunder was the anger—or the laughter—of the gods. Unusual individuals were produced because deities could take human form and cross into reality from time to time for sexual encounters with humans. When people disappeared they were believed to have wandered into a faerie land (such as the Celtic Shi) and lost both memory and the desire to return home.

Fairy tales are usually very brief, complete in themselves, and primarily concerned with common people instead of gods. However, the powerful gods of myths persist in transmuted forms in fairy tales. For example, the gods of

23

Celtic myths and legends became, by Shakespeare's time, the diminutive and mischievous immortals of *A Midsummer Night's Dream.* In the German tales collected by the Brothers Grimm, Rumpelstiltskin and the shoemaker's elves are such transformed deities. In Italy there is the fairy mascaporilla, about whom the children still speak in whispers, and in Ireland are faerie creatures like leprechauns, merrows, banshees, and pookas.

Fairy tales and myths have common characteristics that are often carried down into pure fantasies. These characteristics of fantasy literature include the following:

1. *Epic hero*—a brave, exceptional person, usually of noble lineage, whose coming is often foretold. Epic heroes in myths and legends include Arthur, Thor, Siegfried, Christ, Lancelot, Cuchulain, Boadicea, Achilles, Roland, and Jason; in pure fantasies, Aragorn in *The Lord of the Rings* and Conan in *Conan.*

2. *Unlikely hero*—a person of no previously discovered distinction, a "little person," who performs brave deeds or goes on to great success. Examples of unlikely heroes in fairy tales are the Valiant Tailor, Jack the Giant Killer, Cinderella, and Konbitaro in the Japanese tale "The Dirt Boy"; in pure fantasies, Frodo in *The Lord of the Rings,* Bilbo in *The Hobbit,* Dorothy in *The Wizard of Oz,* and Wart in *The Sword and the Stone.*

3. *The quest*—a journey, often with a company of experts, trying to achieve a specific goal. In ancient mythology, Jason and the Argonauts sail after the golden fleece. In Arthurian myth, the Knights of the Round Table go in search of the Holy Grail. In fairy tales, Jack goes up the beanstalk in search of the giant's treasure; and a mother in the Japanese tale "The Oni's Laughter" goes in search of her daughter who has been kidnapped by an oni (monster). In Tolkien's *The Lord of the Rings,* Frodo and a company go forth to return the ring.

4. *Common motifs—*
   - Transformations into animals and things
   - Disguised royalty and the subsequent transformations and revelations (Odysseus disguised as a beggar, the Frog Prince, the Goose Girl, Aragorn disguised as Strider, Eowyn disguised as Dernhelm)
   - Hunts for precious objects (rings, magic charms)
   - Dark enchanted woods
   - Intermarriages of gods and mortals
   - Poetry and song
   - The passing of a golden age.

5. *Happy ending—*an essential for fairy tales, at least. "And they all lived happily ever after" means that in fairy tales Snow White and Cinderella get their respective princes; Hansel and Gretel return to their parents; and Little Red Riding Hood is rescued by the woodsman. In "On Fairy Stories" Tolkien refers to these concluding moments as the turn, the lifting, the joy of deliverance. But fantasy literature as a whole, although denying universal final defeat, admits the existence of sorrow and failure.

The relationship of the happy ending to the passing of a golden age motif is particularly noteworthy because even though the endings in fantasy literature are usually happy, there is often a great loss experienced as well. At the end of *The Lord of the Rings*, Frodo, Bilbo, and Gandalf depart over the sea, and the elves withdraw from the world of men. *The Once and Future King* tetralogy ends with the destruction of the Round Table. The Icelandic Eddas and the Teutonic Nibelungen tales end with the death of the gods. This sense of loss is well expressed in the Arthurian poem *The Idylls of the King* when Bedivere cries:

> "Ah! my lord Arthur, whither shall I go?
> Where shall I hide my forehead and my eyes?
> For now I see the true old times are dead,
> When every morning brought a noble chance,
> And every chance brought out a noble knight.

The dying Arthur replies from the barge:

> The old order changeth, yielding place to new,
> And God fulfills himself in many ways,
> Lest one good custom should corrupt the world.

This sense of loss is a key to the appeal of fantasy literature, for fantasy literature represents imaginings of magical, "better" days. This sense of loss corresponds to and complements the loss of human innocence that Wordsworth describes.

Suggested Readings

The following list is not, of course, complete or even necessarily representative of fantasy literature, but offers a sampling and a pattern of works suitable for class use. For a more extensive list, see John R. Pfeiffer, *Fantasy and Science Fiction: A Critical Guide* (Palmer Lake, Colorado: Filter Press, 1971). Some grade level divisions and other remarks are made, though many of the works listed are applicable for both elementary and secondary levels. The method of presentation of *Grimms' Fairy Tales* for grade 4 will be different from that for grade 12. Specific analysis, discussion questions, and suggestions for teaching aids for several works in each of the three categories follow the list. The questions are suggested both to foster a better understanding of the stories and fictive techniques and to open children to the wonders of imagination as presented in the stories.

It may be valuable in some cases to incorporate the myths, fairy tales, and fantasies typical of the cultural background of the students and their community, or of an individual student, and discuss and discover similarities and differences with those suggested in this report. For example, the *Ramayana* and the *Jataka* from Asia, the trickster tales from the North American Indians and from Africa, or Aztec and Inca myths from Central and South America might be both available and useful; or the Japanese, Irish, or Norse myths and tales could be further investigated and developed.

Mythology

Greek

Ovid, *Metamorphoses:* II (The Story of Phaeton); VIII (The Death of Icarus); X (Pygmalion and Galatea); XI (Midas and the Golden Touch). Homer, *Odyssey:* X.

Arthurian

Thomas Malory, *Morte d'Arthur:* I, 2–3 (Arthur pulls sword from stone, finds Excalibur); VI, 7 (Sir Bedivere returns Excalibur to the Lady of the Lake).

Celtic

The Mabinogion. "Pwyll, Prince of Dyfed" (for secondary grades)

Norse

Snorri Sturluson, *The Prose Edda:* "The Deluding of Gylfi" (for secondary grades and beyond)

Japanese

"The Woman Who Came Down from Heaven"

Fairy Tales

Grimms' Fairy Tales (German)

"The Fisherman and His Wife"
"The Elves and the Shoemaker"
"Hansel and Gretel"
"The Frog Prince"
"The Blue Light"
"The Five Servants"

Norwegian

"East of the Sun and West of the Moon"
"Billy Goats Gruff"

Japanese

"The Dirt Boy"
"The Oni's Laughter"

The Blue Fairy Book by Andrew Lang

(This, as well as the other color fairy books by Lang, is good source material for fairy tales of all types from a number of cultures.)
"The Princess on the Glass Hill"
"Jack the Giant Killer"

Pure Fantasy

Elementary Grades

Hans Christian Andersen, "The Red Shoes"
_____, "Thumbelina"
James M. Barrie, *Peter Pan*
Frank L. Baum, *The Wizard of Oz*
Lewis Carroll, *Alice's Adventures in Wonderland*
_____, *Through the Looking Glass and What Alice Found There*
Carlo Collodi, *Pinocchio*
Kenneth Grahame, *The Wind in the Willows*
_____, *The Reluctant Dragon*
Rudyard Kipling, *Just So Stories*
Ursula K. LeGuin, *The Wizard of Earthsea*
C. S. Lewis, the Narnia series
Hugh Lofting, *Dr. Doolittle Tales*
George MacDonald, *The Princess and the Goblin*
Antoine de Saint-Exupery, *The Little Prince*
J. R. R. Tolkien, *The Hobbit*
E. B. White, *Charlotte's Web*
_____, *Stuart Little*
T. H. White, *The Sword and the Stone*

Secondary Grades (And Beyond)

Peter S. Beagle, *The Last Unicorn*
Beowulf

James Branch Cabell, *Jurgen*
———, *The Cream of the Jest*
Lord Dunsany, *The King of Elfland's Daughter*
H. Rider Haggard, *She*
Robert E. Howard, *Conan*
C. S. Lewis, The Space Trilogy
H. P. Lovecraft, *The Dream Quest of Unknown Kallath*
Anne McCaffrey, *Dragonflight*
William Morris, *The Wood Beyond the World*
James Stephens, *The Crock of Gold*
J. R. R. Tolkien, *The Lord of the Rings*
Sylvia Townsend-Warner, *Kingdoms of Elfin*
T. H. White, *The Once and Future King*

Myths

The myths of ancient Greece are well known and have reappeared in virtually every form of literature. Myths of other cultures—for example, American Indian, Afro-American, Celtic, Norse, Southeast Asian, Japanese, Chinese—have also been influential in literature and are also available in various versions for classroom use. Northrop Frye argues that all literature is a continuation of the archetypes established in myth. Myths could indeed fill an entire course themselves, but are suggested here as an introduction to otherworldliness.

Greek Myth

Phaeton

An effective introduction to myth is the Greek story of Phaeton, which was retold in Ovid's *Metamorphoses* (Penguin Books, 1955, pp. 50–59) and is available in many more recent versions (though these should be chosen carefully since many lack the benefit of the flavor of antiquity). Basically, it is the story of Apollo's son who obtains permission from his father to drive the fiery chariot across the sky (the Greek con-

FANTASY IN LITERATURE

ception of the sun). Phaeton's inexperience and the horses' realization of this cause the chariot to come too close to the earth. In order to save the earth, Zeus, father of the gods, strikes Phaeton from the chariot with a thunderbolt.

Important to a course in fantasy literature are the descriptions of Apollo's function as the sun god, especially his instructions to Phaeton on how to drive the chariot. The character of Apollo was created by Greek imagination to explain the appearance of the sun. (To expand this point of how myth was universally used to explain natural phenomena, sun myths from other cultures might be referred to or included here, such as Yi the Archer from the Chinese Yellow Emperor cycle.) Once this point is established, other portions of the story can be seen as explanations of other features of nature: Phaeton's coming too close to the earth caused dark skinned people as well as the deserts and the dry land; and weeping willows are the daughters of the sun who were transformed while weeping for Phaeton (Ovid's description of this transformation is quite comic). It is important for students to realize that these explanations developed into a complete fanciful, magical other world in which gods roamed the lands and the skies, controlling the destiny of humanity.

The most obvious fantasy literature motif in this story is transformation. Also apparent in the story are situations that are universal and that will seem familiar even to very young students: a child asking a parent for something unreasonable; that same child biting off more than she/he can chew; and a family grieving at a death.

Questions for discussion

1. What is the relation of Apollo to the sun? What is there about the rising and setting of the sun that could have inspired the Greeks to think of the sun as a fiery chariot riding around the earth? (Note that this is based on the concept that the sun orbits the earth. Students should be reminded of the correct explanation of the sun's apparent motion.)

2. Is there anything in the relationship of Phaeton and Apollo that is familiar in the student's daily life?

3. What is personification? How is it used in the Apollo-Phaeton story? How is it used in other myths?

4. Give examples of transformations in this story, in fantasy literature, and in literature in general.

The Odyssey

Another good example for class use of Greek myth is from the *Odyssey* (Mentor, 1966), although here it should be stressed that this is not a collection of mythic tales, such as the *Metamorphoses*, but rather myths of gods and heroes woven into a single narrative of grand proportions called an epic. In Book X of the *Odyssey*, Odysseus and his men, trying to get home after the Trojan War, visit the Island of the Winds where Aeolus gives Odysseus a bag full of the blustering winds which, so trapped, cannot harm them. Odyseus and his men are almost at home when the men open the bag thinking that it is full of riches—and the winds blow them back where they started. Also in this book, Odysseus and his men are attacked by the Laistrygonians, and they meet the witch Circe who turns the men into swine.

Again, this is a magic land, an other world of gods and witches. Apparent is the Greek use of myth to explain things and thus obtain order: Aeolus is the manager of the winds and lets them out or keeps them in at his discretion or whim. Transformation is illustrated when Circe turns Odysseus's men into swine. Odysseus is an example of the epic hero typical of fantasy literature, a person of superhuman ability—he alone is not charmed by Circe. The entire Odyssey is an example of the quest in fantasy literature since Odysseus and his men are seeking to return home.

This section of the *Odyssey* can also be used to demonstrate various literary techniques such as irony (Odysseus and his men are almost at home but greed keeps them from achieving their quest at the last moment), personification (Aeolus), and even metaphor (Odysseus's men as swine).

Questions for discussion

1. Who is Aeolus? What is there in the winds that could have caused the Greeks to invent him?

2. What type of man is Odysseus? What words would you use to describe him?

3. How would you describe Odysseus's men? Is there any reason why Circe turns them into swine?

King Midas

It might be helpful, both to show how myths have been carried over into modern fantasy literature and also to give younger students a version of a mythic tale that might be easier for them to read, to compare in class Ovid's tale of King Midas in *Metamorphoses* (pp. 248–50) and Nathaniel Hawthorne's retelling of the story, *The Golden Touch* (New York: Whittlesey House, 1959). Hawthorne eliminated Bacchus and put in his place a mysterious stranger. He extended Ovid's details for better dramatic effect; added Midas's daughter to sentimentalize the story; and emphasized the color of gold and its different meanings, the contrasting values of gold and love, and the comic situation of Midas trying to eat golden fish and bread.

Arthurian Myth

As an example of a later mythic tale, students can be assigned readings from Malory's *Morte d'Arthur* (New York: Appleton-Century-Crofts, 1968), the medieval compendium of Arthurian tales. Selections emphasizing magic and the heroic are chapters 2 and 3 of Book I, where Arthur pulls the sword from the stone and gets Excalibur from the Lady of the Lake. Arthur begins as an unlikely hero and then develops into one of epic stature. The magic swords, rings, and other emblems are familiar motifs in fantasy literature. The section of *Morte d' Arthur* in which Excalibur is returned (Book VI, chapter 7) can round out Arthurian myth.

Celtic and Icelandic Myth

Older students should be introduced to exclusively Celtic myth in the *Mabinogion* (New York: E. P. Dutton & Co., 1970) and to Icelandic myth in Snorri Sturluson's *Prose Edda* (Berkeley: University of California Press, 1966).

Japanese Myth

The Japanese "The Woman Who Came Down from Heaven" in *Folktales of Japan* (London: Routledge, & Kegan Paul, Ltd., 1963) is an example of fantasy literature from a nonwestern culture. In this tale a man named Minkeran meets a woman while swimming and playfully takes her kimono. She is a woman from heaven and must stay on earth as long as he keeps her magic kimono. Years later, she finds it and flies to heaven, leaving him behind. She misses Minkeran, however, and gets words to him on how to grow a bamboo tree to heaven (by burying wooden sandals). He climbs to heaven, but once there is given impossible tasks by her father. He fails in his last task and causes a flood in heaven that creates the Milky Way. Minkeran becomes the star Altair, and his wife the star Vega; they are separated by the Milky Way and cry continuously. Class discussion should center around features the story has in common with other fantasy literature—marriage of deities and mortals, the unlikely hero trying to achieve impossible tasks, and the attempt to explain natural phenomena (the Milky Way, the stars, and the rains at the season when Altair and Vega are prominent in the sky).

Teaching Aids—Myths

Greek

● Paintings and pictures of sculptures of the ancient gods as well as sky maps showing positions of sun, moon, stars, and constellations can supplement the teaching of the story of Phaeton and other Greek myths.

• A 1955 Paramount film, done by Americans in Italy, was based on the *Odyssey* and called *Ulysses*. It starred Kirk Douglas in the title role, Silvana Mangano as Penelope and Circe, Anthony Quinn, and a cast of Italian actors. The screenplay was by novelist Irwin Shaw, Hollywood screenwriter Ben Hecht, and Franco Brusati, Mario Camerini, Enio de Concini, Ivo Perilli, and Hugh Gray. Camerini directed. For such an international mishmash, the film turned out quite well, heavy on action (the killing of the suitors), modernizations (Ulysses hears in the sirens' songs the voices of Penelope and Telemachus), and compressions of actions. Some actions have been restructured for better dramatic effect (Ulysses's descent into the underworld), but the fantastic-magical elements are transferred intact. Although it is a "Monarch Notes" version of the epic poem, it is reasonably entertaining and workmanlike and could be an appropriate followup to Greek myth.

Arthurian

• Sections of the Tennyson version of the myths have been recorded: *Idylls of the King: Lancelot and Elaine and the Passing of Arthur*. Read by Basil Rathbone (Caedmon TC2022).

• Another version, T. H. White's *The Once and Future King*, was made into a musical play, *Camelot*, by Frederick Loewe and Alan Jay Lerner in 1960. This play is easy to read aloud in class. It was made into a rather unfanciful movie (Warner Bros., 1967).

• Other film versions of the Arthurian tales (*Knights of the Round Table*, 1954; *Lancelot and Guenevere*, 1963) also emphasized battles and illicit love rather than magic.

• In teaching about King Arthur, the teacher might include in discussions the whole question of the authenticity of Arthur and Camelot and the many archeological excavations made in Great Britain in attempts to discover the truth. Information and pictures on these digs can be found in *From Caesar to Arthur* by Geoffrey Ashe (London: William Collins Sons & Co., Ltd., 1960) and *The Quest for Arthur's Britain* by Ashe and others (New York: Frederick A. Praeger, Inc., 1968).

Such discussion can also be extended to the historical authenticity of any of the myths discussed.

Fairy Tales

"The Blue Light" (in *Grimms' Fairy Tales* [Puffin Books, 1975], pp. 148–52)

This story is about a soldier who has been turned away without reward by the king he has served and so is forced to do labor for a witch. She sends him to the bottom of a deep well to get her a magical blue light. When he will not give her the light, she lets him fall back down to the bottom and leaves him there. When he lights his pipe with the blue light, a little black dwarf appears who grants his wishes. The soldier's wishes give him revenge against the witch and the king's evil counselors, and gain for him the king's daughter as a wife.

The first aspect of the story to be noted is the use of the unlikely hero: the hero of the story is not a great king or warrior but a wronged common soldier who begs for food, stumbles onto a magic tool, and seeks justice, revenge, and love. Then there is the dark, forbidding woods where the soldier meets the witch, a place of terror because it is full of unknowns, and, as such, is a common fantasy literature motif.

Typical of fairy tales, the magical personages are not gods but a witch, and a dwarf who appears in the manner of the genie from Aladdin's lamp and who serves a function similar to Rumpelstiltskin, the Fairy Godmother in "Cinderella," the Cheshire Cat in *Alice's Adventures in Wonderland,* (and perhaps the robots in science fiction). The witch and the dwarf establish the other world. Also familiar is the motif of the princess dropping peas to leave a trail, which appears in several fairy tales, including "Hansel and Gretel."

There is a naturalness about the story, even though it deals with witches and magic dwarfs. No explanation is given for the witch or the dwarf or the blue light. They are just part of the story, something to be accepted and expected in the land of faerie. In keeping with this naturalness is the way the soldier discovers the magic dwarf: by lighting his pipe.

The soldier's revenge raises a question of morality. The soldier has the dwarf bring the king's daughter to him in her sleep and later has the dwarf "kill, slay, or put to flight all these people." But the king's life is spared; the witch is not harmed when she is placed at the bottom of the well, nor was the soldier when the witch dropped him down the same well. Violence is suggested, but there is no pain or gore in this fairy tale, and the soldier's revenge seems justified and not excessive.

Questions for discussion

1. What type of man is the soldier—good? bad? Justify this by his actions.

2. Is anyone hurt in this story? Why or why not?

3. What other fictional characters can you think of that are like the dwarf?

4. Would you say a lot of the action (the part with the king's daughter) is sketchy or hurried? Or is there a reason for this lack of detail?

"The Fisherman and His Wife" (in *Grimms' Fairy Tales* [Puffin Books, 1975], pp. 23–28)

This tale contains the fantasy literature elements of an unlikely hero(s) (a fisherman and his wife), transformation, a disguised king (the fish), poetry, and magic wishes. A fisherman catches and releases an enchanted fish and, at his wife's prompting, asks it for favors. The fish gives them a cottage, then a stone castle, then makes the wife king, emperor, and pope. When the wife wants to rule the sun and moon, the fish returns the fisherman and his wife to their former state. Again, the magic is accepted and not explained.

Of interest are the literary techniques apparent in the tale: the use of repetition as the fisherman's song is repeated over and over for different requests, and the pathetic fallacy as the water and sky become darker and darker as the wife's wishes get wilder and wilder.

Questions for discussion

1. Why does the fisherman's wife ask for more and more? Is she wrong in doing this? What would you ask for if a magic fish would grant your wishes?

2. What patterns are there in the story?

3. Who is the fish? He talks so little. How do we know what he thinks or feels?

4. Discuss the ending. Does it come too suddenly? Is it the happy ending typical of fairy tales?

5. Define pathetic fallacy in relation to the story.

"The Five Servants" (in *Grimms' Fairy Tales* [Puffin Books, 1975], pp. 232–38)

This fairy tale is a brief and concise illustration of a particular fantasy literature characteristic: the quest with a company of experts. This particular version is from the Brothers Grimm, though the basic plot is also found in tales of most other cultures.

A young prince, going to compete for the hand of a beautiful princess, meets in the woods a fat man, a man who has acute hearing, a very tall man, a man who is always cold, and a man who has very sharp eyes. Their special skills are utilized to pass the tests the old queen contrives. For instance, they retrieve a ring the queen dropped in the sea by having the fat man drink the sea and the tall man stoop to get the ring. The princess is not happy with all this and arranges her own test, which the company passes. The prince tells the princess that he is really a swineherd and has her feed the swine. Later she finds out that her new husband is a prince after all.

The banding together of experts into a company or fellowship is a literary technique that stretches from the *Odyssey* and the *Voyage of the Argo* to *The Lord of the Rings, That Hideous Strength, The Wizard of Oz* and to such nonfantasy works as Hemingway's *For Whom the Bell Tolls,* the film *The Seven Samurai* (American version, *The Magnificent Seven*), and the TV series *Mission Impossible.* It is particularly characteristic of fantasy literature, one that adds strength to the defense against magical evil and makes it possible to include characters with a variety of magical skills.

Fantasy literature motifs in the story are the dark woods, the hunt for a ring, and the disguised prince (which has a double twist).

Older students might compare "The Five Servants" to Arthurian and Celtic myth in the use of exaggerated phrases (the young prince is ill for seven years) and of various trials (comparable to the ritual in the quest for the Holy Grail).

Questions for discussion

1. Discuss the repetition in "The Five Servants." Does it serve any effect?

2. Does the princess deserve the trick the prince plays on her?

3. Who are the five servants? Why do they follow the prince? Where do they go when it is all over?

4. Discuss the old queen and compare her with other characters in fantasy literature.

5. Imagine the story ending with the prince's death. How should the story be different to lead to this end?

"East of the Sun and West of the Moon" (in P. C. Asbjörnsen and Jorgen E. Moe, *East of the Sun and West of the Moon* [New York: Macmillan, 1953])

This Norwegian tale is about the daughter of a poor husbandman. A white bear comes to the door and promises the husbandman riches if he will give his daughter to the bear. After some discussion, the daughter agrees and goes off with the bear to a magic castle where she is given anything she wants. Each night a man comes into her room and lies by her side (it is the bear who has put off his beast shape). When the daughter returns home for a visit, her mother gives her a candle. When she lights it to see the man, he tells her that he is an enchanted prince who has been bewitched by his step-mother. Since the girl has violated his trust, the prince must marry another princess with a nose "three ells long" at his mother's castle that is "east of the sun and west of the moon." The girl goes in search of the castle, encounters three old hags, and enlists the aid of the East, West, South, and finally the North Wind to find the castle. Once there, the girl and the prince engineer a plot so that the prince will marry only the woman who can wash his shirt.

This story contains many fantasy literature elements: transformation, a quest, an unlikely hero (in this case a young girl), a disguised prince, and a happy ending. Nature is personified. Again, there is a naturalness about the otherworldliness. The white bear knocks at the window and say, "Good evening to you!" to which the husbandman replies, "The same to you." The girl converses with the winds and unquestioningly mounts their backs. She completes the quest not by battle or virtue but by washing a shirt.

The story is very reminiscent of "Beauty and the Beast," and the Psyche and Cupid myth. Like "Beauty and the Beast," the story can be seen as that of a young girl's matura-tion into a woman through love.

Questions for discussion

1. Discuss the "magic" in the story.

2. What does the story tell us about lying?

3. What is your reaction to the girl's mother and father?

4. Is there any reason why it is a white bear and not some other animal?

5. Discuss repetitions in the story. What purpose do they serve, if any?

6. Describe the different winds as characters.

7. How many "tests" are there in the story? How are they different?

Teaching Aids—Fairy Tales

• Some of *Grimms' Fairy Tales* have been recorded in *Tom Thumb, Rumpelstiltskin, and Other Fairy Tales*. Read by Joseph Schildkraut (Caedmon TC1062).

• *The Wonderful World of the Brothers Grimm* (1962) is ostensibly a biographical film about the two brothers, but it includes dramatizations of "The Dancing Princess," "The Cobbler and the Elves," and "The Singing Bone."

• Walt Disney cartoons of fairy tales include *Snow White and the Seven Dwarfs* (1938), *Cinderella* (1950), and *Sleeping Beauty* (1958).

• Teachers should be aware of the possibility of class dramatizations of fairy tales. Many children's versions are available, or the students can create the plays themselves. The tales are short; and some, like "The Fisherman and His Wife," contain extensive dialogue. In the late 1960s, the Story Theatre dramatized fairy tales on Broadway with production values similar to those available in a classroom—modern dress, no scenery, make-believe props.

Pure Fantasy

Through the Looking Glass by Lewis Carroll (*Alice's Adventures in Wonderland and Through the Looking Glass*, 1871; reprint ed. Penguin, 1971)

Through the Looking Glass is a sequel to the more familiar *Alice's Adventures in Wonderland*. Common to both are the character of Alice, the kitten Dinah, the king's messengers (the March Hare and the Mad Hatter), the use of a dream ending, poetry, the theme of identity, and various fantasy literature characteristics. Like *Alice's Adventures in Wonderland*, it is a pleasant, amiable fantasy that is inherently complex and serious without being obtuse. Like *Alice's Adven-*

tures in Wonderland, it plays it safe as fantasy by couching its narrative within a dream.

But *Through the Looking Glass* is actually a much more structured tale than *Alice's Adventures in Wonderland* because it uses a chessboard for its other world setting and a chess game for describing Alice's adventures. The faerie world of *Through the Looking Glass* is a microcosm of reality:

> I declare it's marked out just like a large chessboard! . . . It's a huge game of chess that's being played—all over the world—if this *is* the world at all, you know. (pp. 213–14)

The chess game, described in a list of moves at the story's start, emphasizes changes of place—but within a dream framework. Examples are the train ride and the transformation of the queen in the woods to a sheep in a store to the sheep in a rowboat. "Things flow about so here!" says Alice (p. 260).

Another structuring element in *Through the Looking Glass* is the mirror motif. Because through the looking glass is a land where things are reversed, the poem "Jabberwocky" is printed backwards, Alice has to walk backwards to meet the Red Queen, and one whispers by shouting and runs to stay in the same place. This looking glass land is full of puns, of plays on the alternate meanings of words.

The mirror motif, by concentrating on images, strengthens what is probably the most important theme in the story: the identity theme. Tweedledum and Tweedledee tell Alice that she is only something the Red King is dreaming—only an image in his mind, despite Alice's protests that she *is* real. Later, in the woods where things have no names, Alice forgets who she is. In order for Alice to complete her journey and become queen, she has to learn to confirm her identity and assert herself.

Many characteristics of fairy tales and myths are present in *Through the Looking Glass.* Dinah, who may or may not have been the Red Queen, is a black cat, and black cats have long been associated with witches and magic. There are many fantastic characters. The woods are forbidding and gloomy like the woods in *Grimms' Fairy Tales* and the Shi in Celtic myths. Alice's chessboard journey is a form of quest, and "Jabberwocky" is a quest poem about the slaying of a hideous beast. Alice is an unlikely hero. There are many poems and songs in *Through the Looking Glass*, which are not parodies like those in *Alice's Adventures in Wonderland* but songs and poems for their own sake.

Although the dream ending does lessen the impact of the imaginary, chessboard other world, *Through the Looking Glass* is a good example of fantasy literature as defined in this report; and its complicated texture, with its ideas weaving and interrelating through use of the mirror motif, are typified in the Red King's dream of Alice who is dreaming of the Red King who is dreaming of Alice. . .

Questions for discussion

1. What is the purpose of the chessboard introduction? Do you have to know chess to understand it?

2. Is the story a dream? If so, why? Does this weaken the story as fantasy literature? What is the importance of the dream idea in the story?

3. Does Alice change at the end? Look at the closing poem.

4. Talk about Alice as traveler (How does she react to her adventures?) and as someone on a quest.

5. Discuss the language in "Jabberwocky." How do the nonsense words relate to the real words? What do they mean?

Teaching Aids—Through the Looking Glass

Recordings

● *Alice Through the Looking Glass* (RCA Mono LOC-1130; Stereo LSO-1130). This soundtrack recording of a 1966 musical television special stars Judi Rolin as Alice, Jimmy Durante as Humpty Dumpty, Jack Palance as the Jabberwock, Ricardo Montalban as the White King, Nanette Fabray as the White Queen, Roy Castle as Lester the Jester, and the Smothers Brothers as Tweedledum and Tweedledee. It is a typical Broadway-like treatment—adding characters, oversimplifying the original. But it may be helpful because it can be a tuneful complement to class instruction and an illustration of what *Through the Looking Glass* might be like with a more conventional structure.

Through the Looking Glass. Read by Joan Greenwood, Stanley Holloway, and a cast of eight (Caedmon TC 1098).

Drama

- An off-Broadway version of *Alice's Adventures in Wonderland* was presented in 1970, directed by André Gregory, utilizing movement and emphasizing the psychological elements of the original. Students could dramatize *Through the Looking Glass* as they did fairy tales, in a Story-Theatre method of presentation.

Films

- Alice in Wonderland (Paramount, 1933) combined elements of *Alice's Adventures in Wonderland* and *Through the Looking Glass* with an all-star cast. It may seem dated by today's standards. Other versions are a 1950 British film blending puppets and live action; the Walt Disney cartoon version; and a 1972 British film starring Peter Sellers.

The Crock of Gold by James Stephens (1912; reprint ed., Colliers, 1967)

This modern fantasy, set in faerie Ireland, uses characters from Celtic myths and fairy tales as well as from Greek mythology.

It is a story about a philosopher (and his wife who is the Thin Woman of Inis Magrath) who gives advice to Meehawl MacMurrachu so that he is able to find the leprechauns' pot of gold. To get it back the leprechauns kidnap the philosopher's two children and tell the Greek god Pan, who has come to Ireland, to entice Caitilin, MacMurrachu's daughter. To untangle these complications, the philosopher goes in search of Angus Óg, the Irish deity. Later the Thin Woman goes on a similar journey. Caitilin finally rejects the pure sensuality of Pan and choses Angus Og not only because he is of her native land but also because he wants her to complement him and to continue to grow towards wisdom. By the end of the story the children as well as all other imprisoned creatures are released and all the mortal and immortal inhabitants of faerie Ireland return "dancing and singing, to the country of the gods. . ."

Unlike *Alice's Adventures in Wonderland* or *Through the Looking Glass,* and more like myths and fairy tales, *The Crock of Gold* does not end as a dream. Rather it begins and ends without explanation in an obviously faerie other world where leprechauns roam—and can call the police—and asses talk to spiders. In many places the story is wildly improbable, though it has its own inherent logic (as befits a story with a philosopher for a main character), and a naturalness of its otherworldliness. The theme of complementary opposites runs throughout: reason and emotion (the philosopher and his wife), male and female, mortal and immortal, insider and outsider (Óg and Pan), thought and intuition. It contains the story of a young girl growing to maturity through love, like "Beauty and the Beast."

There are many fantasy literature characteristics in *The Crock of Gold:* faerie creatures, intermarriage of gods and mortals, dark woods, a search for a precious object (the crock of gold), and a quest (the philosopher's and the Thin Woman's journeys in search of Angus Óg).

The Crock of Gold is best suited to older students not only because of the nakedness of Caitilin and Pan but also because the story is full of philosophy as well as nonsense and much of the humor is quite subtle.

Questions for discussion

1. What about *The Crock of Gold* is like a "tall tale"?

2. How is *The Crock of Gold* different from *Through the Looking Glass?*

3. What are the different quests in the story?

4. The philosopher is called only by his title. Is that fitting?

5. Discuss the ending. What does it signify—heaven? The end of the world?

Teaching Aids—The Crock of Gold

• The 1947 musical *Finian's Rainbow* (Berkeley Medalion, 1968) was inspired, without credit, by *The Crock of Gold*. The location has been moved to Kissitucky, U.S.A., and it concerns an Irishman named Finian who comes to America with a leprechaun's pot of gold. He is pursued by a leprechaun named Óg (from Angus Óg).

The Lord of the Rings by J. R. R. Tolkien (1954–55; reprint ed., Ballantine, 1965)

This work is at once essential for any study of fantasy literature and also so epic in its length and scope that it is difficult to cover adequately in any curriculum. It is surely not beyond the comprehension of younger children—for it is simply written and well told—though the length of *The Lord of the Rings* (*LOTR*) makes *The Hobbit*, an earlier book that begins the story of the *LOTR*, preferable for them. In many ways, *The Hobbit* is an early draft of the *LOTR* with Bilbo in place of Frodo.

LOTR is a veritable storehouse of motifs and parallels of fantasy literature. It draws on Greek myth and epic, Icelandic and German myth, *Beowulf*, and various fairy tales. Simply, the trilogy concerns a young hobbit (or halfling) named Frodo who, given a magic ring of terrible powers by Bilbo (who got it from Gollum in *The Hobbit*), goes on a quest to return it to its source while various forces and individuals try to get the ring from him.

Fantasy literature characteristics include the following: transformations (the Gollum, once a young hobbit, has turned into a hideous creature because of his lust for the ring; Aragorn is a prince disguised as strider); woods and animate nature (Old Man Willow; the Ents, Tom Bombadil); a quest with a band of experts; an epic hero (Aragorn); an unlikely hero (Frodo and all the hobbits); the Fisher or stricken king of Arthurian legend (Frodo, Theoden); intermarriage of mortal and immortal (Aragorn and Arwen); the use of poetry and song; and, of course, the hunt for a ring or precious object.

LOTR is perhaps the perfect example of the complete sub-creation of an other world. From its pseudo-historical prologue, which presents the appearance of reality, the story is written as a factual account. The hobbits are our entry into this faerie world. There is no apology for them or explanation. They are our reference to reality among the more fanciful creatures in the trilogy. But since they are also fantasy creations, the hobbits are both reality and fantasy, or real unreality—the essence of fantasy literature.

The attempt to make the *LOTR* seem true continues in the extensive appendixes, vocabularies, and maps (analogous to but more elaborate than Carroll's in *Through the Looking Glass*).

There are various themes binding the trilogy together. First, there is the theme of responsibility. Frodo, the unlikely hero, makes a hero-like decision to go on the quest, and finally, calmly, and heroically accepts his fate. (The ring has, in a way, spoiled him for life, so with Gandalf and Bilbo—and like Arthur, he goes over the seas, never to return.) Second, there is the theme of good versus evil. Those who are affected by the ring include good persons (Saruman and Boromir) as well as bad (Sauron). The ring even has an effect on Frodo (at the last moment at the Crack of Doom he is unable to give up the ring). This illustrates then, the matter of degrees of evil—Frodo must use the ring at times in the name of good, although each time it weakens him—and it includes a comment about the nature of evil—Sauron's mistake is that it is beyond his understanding that anyone would destroy the ring. The result of evil is loss—the end of the Third Age and all its wonder.

A third theme is that of life versus death. Tom Bombadil is a nature spirit filled with the joy of living. Gondor, on the other hand, is a symbol of a dying city. The time sequence of the trilogy is from winter to spring—death to life. Fourth is the theme of fate which is related to the theme of life—Frodo was meant to get the ring; Gollum has his inevitable part to play. Finally, there is the theme of love. This includes romantic love (Sam and Rose, Aragorn and Arwen, Faramir and Eowyn), courtly love (Gimli's defense of Galadriel's name), comradeship (the fellowship, Sam and Frodo—similar to Achilles and Patrocles, or David and Jonathan), and even Gollum *loves* his precious ring.

LOTR does have flaws. The women characters are very stiff. It is an atypical fantasy in that it is somewhat lacking in humor. Edmund Wilson in a review of the trilogy criticized it because after all the build-up, the destruction of evil (Sauron) is very skimpy; and Sauron, the main antagonist, is never seen.

However, *LOTR* is perhaps the most ambitious pure fantasy existant, a wholehearted attempt to create another world peripherally divorced from reality.

Questions for discussion

1. Discuss Frodo as an unlikely hero and as an epic hero.

2. What type of power does the ring have?

3. Why do we never see Sauron?

4. Is all the poetry alike?

5. What is the purpose of the appendixes, maps, and indexes?

6. Who is Tom Bombadil?

Teaching Aid—The Lord of the Rings

• *The Road Goes Ever on: A Song Cycle* (music by Donald Swann) (Ballantine, 1968). Tolkien is reported to have approved of these song treatments based on songs in the *LOTR*. They seem mannered and "recitalish," though they are good to have so that the students can hear how the songs sound when sung.

C. S. Lewis, *Space Trilogy—Out of the Silent Planet; Perelandra: That Hideous Strength* (New York: Macmillan, 1971—each published separately)

This trilogy is of interest for several reasons, especially as a conclusion to a course on fantasy literature. First, Lewis was a colleague of Tolkien's and, consequently, their works merit comparison. Second, the trilogy straddles the line between science fiction and pure fantasy, being science fiction in its outer-space setting but seeming more fantasy than science fiction in its concentration on mythic characters rather than scientific reference. Third, the trilogy uses many mythic characters and situations. Teachers should be aware, however, that some portions of the book are didactic reworkings of Christian themes.

Out of the Silent Planet (1941) concerns a philologist named Ransom who is kidnapped by two unscrupulous scientists (Weston and Devine) to the planet Malacandra or Mars. The scientists plan conquest of the planet, but Ransom, on his own, encounters various creatures—sorns, hross, and Oyarsa—and finds the latter to be superior beings, similar to angels.

Perelandra (1944) finds Ransom traveling to the planet Perelandra or Venus where he encounters a new Eve about to undergo temptation. He and Weston, who takes the part of the Devil, do battle for her. Ransom wins, though he is badly wounded. Note that all science fiction elements have left the trilogy—for example, Weston travels to Perelandra via a supernaturally sped coffin.

That Hideous Strength (1946) is Lewis's reworking of Arthurian myth, which never ended since it was prophesied that Arthur and Merlin would return. Merlin does return in *That Hideous Strength*. Ransom is now identified as the wounded man or the Fisher King, another carry-over from Arthurian myth. Ransom and his company defeat an evil organization called N. I.C.E., headed by Devine. The book is climaxed by the descent of all the gods.

Questions for discussion

1. How does Lewis try to present the action of *Out of the Silent Planet* as real?

2. Why is the new Eve in *Perelandra* green?

3. How much science fiction is there in *Perelandra*?

4. Is there much suspense in *Perelandra*?

5. Discuss the subtitle of *That Hideous Strength*—"A Modern Fairy Tale for Grown-Ups."

6. Compare Lewis and Tolkien in their approach to evil.

7. List the myths Lewis revives and reworks.

8. Does the combination of genres—pure fantasy, science fiction, allegory, Christian writing—affect the flow of each novel?

9. Discuss the relevance of this advertisement for Lewis's *That Hideous Strength:*

THAT HIDEOUS STRENGTH
A Modern Fairy Tale
The Exciting Conclusion To
THE SPACE TRILOGY
starring
Mark and Jane
Special Guest Star
RANSOM
With Cameo Appearances by
THE OYARSA OF THE HEAVENS
and
MERLIN THE MAGICIAN

Footnotes

Footnotes

1. *The Random House Dictionary of the English Language* (New York: Random House, 1966), p. 515.
2. Samuel Johnson, *Rasselas,* in *Rasselas, Poems, and Selected Poems* (San Francisco: Rinehart Press, 1971) p. 693. [XLIV].
3. Ralph Waldo Emerson, "Experience," *Essays: Second Series* (Philadelphia: David McKay, 1888), p. 69.
4. Eric Klinger, *Structure and Function of Fantasy* (New York: John Wiley & Sons, 1971), pp. 11–12.
5. Elizabeth Leonie Simpson, "A Holistic Approach to Moral Development and Behavior," in *Moral Development and Behavior: Theory, Research and Social Issues,* ed. Thomas Licona (New York: Holt, Rinehart, and Winston, 1976), p. 169.
6. Sigmund Freud, *The Interpretation of Dreams,* ed. and trans. James Strackey (New York: Basic Books, 1959), p. 491.
7. Quoted in Mary Ann Pulaski, "The Rich Rewards of Make Believe," *Psychology Today* (January 1974), p. 68.
8. Jean Piaget, *The Child's Conception of the World* (1929; reprint ed., Totowa, New Jersey: Littlefield, Adams, and Co., 1975), pp. 161-62.
9. Erik H. Erikson, *Childhood and Society* (New York: W. W. Norton & Co., Inc., 1963), p. 209.
10. *Ibid.,* p. 211.
11. Bruno Bettelheim, *The Uses of Enchantment: The Meaning and Importance of Fairy Tales* (New York: Alfred A. Knopf, 1976), p. 7.
12. Carl G. Jung, "Approaching the Unconscious," in *Man and His Symbols,* eds. Carl G. Jung and M. L. von Franz (Garden City, New York: Doubleday, 1964), pp. 44–45.
13. William Wordsworth, "The World Is Too Much With Us," *Wordsworth: Poetical Works* (London: Oxford University Press, 1966), p. 206.
14. Jung, p. 99.
15. William Wordsworth, "Ode on Intimations of Immortality," *Wordsworth: Poetical Works,* p. 460.
16. *Ibid,* p. 461.
17. Mary Ann Pulaski, "The Rich Rewards of Make Believe," *Psychology Today* (January 1974), pp. 70–72.
18. Jerome Bruner, "Play is Serious Business," *Psychology Today* (January 1975), p. 81.
19. Jerome Singer, "Fantasy: The Foundation of Serenity," *Psychology Today* (July 1976), p. 32.

20. Kornei Chukovsky, *From Two to Five* (Berkeley: University of California Press, 1966), p. 184.
21. Kahlil Gibran, "The Goddess of Fantasy," *Thoughts and Meditations* (New York: Citadel, 1960), pp. 74–75.
22. J. R. R. Tolkien, "On Fairy Stories," in *Essays Presented to Charles Williams*, ed. C. S. Lewis (1947; reprint ed. Grand Rapids, Michigan: William B. Eerdmans, 1966), pp. 60–67.
23. *Ibid*, p. 43.
24. It is difficult to reconcile poetry in the definition of fantasy literature. Fantasy literature is seen as a convincing portrayal of a magical or fanciful other world, and poetic speech would seem too artificial for such a portrayal. However, fanciful poetry such as Mother Goose rhymes, like fantasy literature, has both defenders and detractors in childhood education. For a defender, see Anthony Burgess, "Don't Cook Mother Goose," *New York Times Book Review* (November 5, 1967); Burgess argues that these rhymes give children an early exposure to poetry and literary techniques and should prove instrumental in language development.
25. See John Aquino, *Science Fiction as Literature* (Washington, D.C.: National Education Association, 1976).
26. Maria Montessori, *To Educate the Human Potential* (India: Kaakshetia Publications, 1948), p. 16.
27. Walter Kerr, *Tragedy and Comedy* (New York: Simon and Schuster, 1967), p. 204.
28. A. M. Tausch, "Einige Auswirkungen Von Marcheninhalten" [Some Effects of Fairy Tales], *Psychologische Rundschau*, Vol. 18, No. 2, 1967, pp. 104–16.
29. Josette Frank, *Your Child's Reading Today* (Garden City, New York: Doubleday, 1969), p. 123.
30. Isabell Jan, *On Children's Literature* (New York: Schoken Books, 1969), p. 75.
31. Bettelheim, p. 6.
32. Joseph L. Henderson, "Ancient Myths and Modern Man," in *Man and His Symbols*, eds. Carl G. Jung and M. L. Franz (Garden City, New York: Doubleday, 1964), pp. 44–45.
33. Lewis Carroll, *Alice's Adventures in Wonderland* and *Through the Looking Glass* (Baltimore, Maryland: Penguin, 1971), pp. 243–45.
34. C. S. Lewis, "On Three Ways of Writing for Children," in *Of Other Worlds: Essays and Stories*, ed. Walter Hooper (New York: Harcourt, Brace, and World, 1965), p. 29.
35. G. K. Chesterton, "The Ethics of Elfland," in *Flights: Readings in Magic, Mysticism, Fantasy, and Myth* (New York: Harcourt, Brace, Jovanovich, 1974), p. 180.

36. Bettelheim, p. 6.
37. Lewis, p. 29.
38. Tolkien, p. 72.
39. Lewis, p. 30.
40. Bettelheim, p. 7.
41. Usually, however, fantasy literature is convincing on its own terms. Tolkien provides word lists and chronologies in *The Lord of the Rings* trilogy. Carroll frames *Through the Looking Glass* within the structure of a chessgame, and both *Alice's Adventures in Wonderland* and *Through the Looking Glass* have a consistent, mad, rigid logic.
42. Bettelheim, p. 117.
43. Tolkien, pp. 61–62.
44. Northrop Frye, *The Educated Imagination* (Bloomington, Indiana: Indiana University Press, 1964), p. 120.
45. *Ibid.*, pp. 110–112.

Selected References

Selected References

Aquino, John. *Science Fiction as Literature.* Washington, D.C.: National Education Association, 1976.

Bettelheim, Bruno. *The Uses of Enchantment: The Meaning and Importance of Fairy Tales.* New York: Alfred A. Knopf, 1976.

Bodem, Marguerite M. "The Role of Fantasy in Children's Reading," *Elementary English* (April 1975), pp. 470–71.

Bruner, Jerome. "Play Is Serious Business," *Psychology Today* (January 1975), pp. 81–83.

Byers, Neil B. "Porridge for Goldilocks," *Elementary English* (December 1948), pp. 501–05.

Carter, Lin. *Imaginary Worlds.* New York: Ballantine Books, 1973.

A Curriculum for English. Grades 1–6. Units 1–70. Lincoln, Nebraska: University of Nebraska Curriculum Development Center, 1967.

Freyberg, Joan T. "Hold High the Cardboard Sword," *Psychology Today* (February 1975), pp. 63–64.

Frye, Northrop. *The Educated Imagination.* Bloomington, Indiana: Indiana University Press, 1964.

Gibran, Kahlil. "The Goddess of Fantasy," *Thoughts and Meditations.* New York: Citadel, 1960. pp. 74–75.

Green, Roger Lancelyn. *Tellers of Tales.* London: Edmund Ward Ltd., 1953.

Harms, Jeanne McLain. *Children's Responses to Fantasy in Relation to Their Stages of Intellectual Development,* unpublished dissertation, Ohio State University, 1972.

Higgins, James E. *Beyond Words: Mystical Fancy in Children's Literature.* New York: Teachers College Press, 1970.

"The Hobbit Habit," *Time* (July 15, 1966), pp. 48; 51.

Holland, Norman N. *The Dynamics of Literary Response.* New York: Oxford University Press, 1968.

Jung, Carl G., et al. *Man and His Symbols*, edited by Carl G. Jung and M. L. von Franz. Garden City, New York: Doubleday, 1964.

Lewis, C. S. *Of Other Worlds: Essays and Stories*, edited by Walter Hooper. New York: Harcourt, Brace, and World, 1965.

Massey, Sara. "The Importance of Fantasy," *Today's Education* (January-February 1975), pp. 42–43.

Myers, Susan L. *Children's Literature.* Alamosa, Colorado: Adams State College of Colorado, 1972.

Olson, Paul A. *A Curriculum Study Center in English. Final Report.* Lincoln, Nebraska: University of Nebraska Curriculum Development Center, 1967.

Paskanzer, Susan Cornell. "A Case for Fantasy," *Elementary English* (April 1975), pp. 472–75.

Piaget, Jean. *The Child's Conception of the World,* 1929. Reprint. Totowa, New Jersey: Littlefield, Adams, and Co., 1975.

Pulaski, Mary Ann. "The Rich Rewards of Make Believe," *Psychology Today* (January 1974), pp. 70–72.

Singer, Jerome L., "Fantasy: The Foundation of Serenity," *Psychology Today* (July 1976), pp. 32–34:37.

Tolkien, J. R. R. "On Fairy-Stories," in *Essays Presented to Charles Williams*, edited by C. S. Lewis, 1947. Reprint. Grand Rapids, Michigan: William B. Eerdmans, 1966.

Additional Resource Materials

Following are some of the many books and articles available to assist you. In addition, some research in your local library or in the professional teaching materials compiled by your school or local education association should provide further useful references.

Andrews, E. G. "The Development of Imagination in the Pre-School Child." *University of Iowa Studies of Character* 3 No. 4; 1930.

Ashmore, J. "Imagination and Its Educational Significance: Creative Activity of the Mind." *Journal of General Education* 25:95–102; July 1973.

Borman, E. G. "Fantasy of Rhetorical Vision: The Rhetorical Criticism of Social Reality." *Quarterly Journal of Speech* 58:396–407; December 1972.

Chethik, M., and Fast, I. "Function of Fantasy in the Borderline Child." *American Journal of Orthopsychiatry* 40:756–65; October 1970.

Cooper, John C. *Fantasy and the Human Spirit.* New York: Seabury, 1975.

Crossley, R. "Education and Fantasy." *College English* 37:281–93; November 1975.

Davidson, D. A. "Sword and Sorcery Fiction: An Annotated Book List." *English Journal* 61:43–51; January 1972.

"Fantasy and Science: By Children." *Elementary English* 52:620–30; May 1975.

Ferman, E. L. *Best from Fantasy and Science Fiction: A Special 25th Anniversary Anthology*. New York: Ace Books, 1977.

Fletcher, Angus. *Allegory: The Theory of a Symbolic Mode*. Ithaca, N.Y.: Cornell University Press, 1970.

Gove, Philip B. *Imaginary Voyage in Prose Fiction*. New York: Octagon Books, 1975.

Hamilton, V. "Literature, Creativity and Imagination." *Childhood Education* 49:307–10; March 1973.

Harms, J. M. "Children's Responses to Fantasy in Literature." *Language Arts* 52:942–46; October 1975.

Hassell, Jon. *Fantasy Voyage Through Outer Space*. Racine, WI: Western Publishing, 1974.

Hatfield, David D. *Fantasy in Flight: Man's Early Attempts to Fly, 1500 B.C.–1900 A.D.*, edited by C. Burton Cosgrove. Glendale, CA: Aviation Book Co., 1974.

Jacobs, K. "Language Arts: Producing a Class Storybook: Activity for K-3rd Grade." *Elementary English* 49:219; February 1972.

Jones, Richard M. *Fantasy and Feeling in Education*. New York: Harper & Row, 1970.

Kelley, G. F. "Guided Fantasy as a Counseling Technique with Youth." *Journal of Counseling Psychology* 19:355–61; September 1972.

Kelley, Leo P. *Fantasy: The Literature of the Marvelous*. New York: McGraw Hill, 1973.

Khatena, J. "Creative Imagination and What We Can Do to Stimulate." *Gifted Child Quarterly* 21:84–97; Spring 1977.

——. "Creative Imagination Imagery: Where Is It Going?" *Journal of Creative Behavior* 10 No. 3:189–92; 1976.

Larson, Ross. *Fantasy and Imagination in the Mexican Narrative*. Tempe: Arizona State University, Center for Latin American Studies, 1977.

Livingston, M. C. "Literature, Creativity and Imagination." *Childhood Education* 48:356–61; April 1972.

McHenry, R. E., and Shouksmith, G. A. "Creativity, Visual Imagination, and Suggestibility: Their Relationship in a Group of 10-Year-Old Children." *The British Journal of Educational Psychology* 40:154–60; June 1970.

Murphy, Richard. *Imaginary Worlds: Notes on a New Curriculum.* New York: Teachers and Writers Collaborative, 1974.

Peppin, Brigid. *Fantasy: The Golden Age of Fantastic Illustration.* New York: New American Library, 1976.

Petrosky, A. R. "Effects of Reality Perception and Fantasy on Response to Literature: Two Case Studies." *Research in the Teaching of English* 10:239–58; Winter 1976.

Pfeiffer, John R. *Fantasy and Science Fiction: A Critical Guide.* Palmer Lake, CO: Filter Press, 1971.

Pulaski, M. A. S. "Play as a Function of Toy Structure and Fantasy Predisposition." *Child Development* 41:531–37; June 1970.

Rosenberg, M. "Releasing the Creative Imagination." *Journal of Creative Behavior* 10 No. 3:203–09; 1976.

Sartre, Jean-Paul. *Imaginations: A Psychological Critique.* Ann Arbor: University of Michigan Press, 1972.

Schwartz, E. M. "Family Romance Fantasy in Children Adopted in Infancy." *Child Welfare* 49:386–91; July 1970.

Spitze, G. S. "Fantasizing and Poetry Construction in Pre-Schoolers." *Childhood Education* 46:283–84+; February 1970.

Summerfield, G. "Making Room for Fantasy." *Times Educational Supplement* 3179:26–27; May 7, 1976.

Whitaker, Stephen P. *Imagination and Fancy in Nineteenth Century Literature.* Folcroft, PA: Folcroft Library Editions, 1912.

Wimsatt, James I. *Allegory and Mirror: Tradition and Structure in Middle English Literature.* Indianapolis, IN: Pegasus, Bobbs-Merrill Co., 1970.